IN CELEBRATION OF

WINTER

A Book of Seasonal Indulgences

IN CELEBRATION OF

WIN

TER

A Book of Seasonal Indulgences

BY HELEN THOMPSON

KODANSHA AMERICA

New York • Tokyo • London

For my mother, Louise Thompson, and my mother-in-law, Lavinia Lohrmann

Kodansha America, Inc.
114 Fifth Avenue, New York, New York 10011, U.S.A.

Kodansha International Ltd.
17-14 Otowa 1-chome, Bunkyo-ku, Tokyo 112, Japan

Published in 1997 by Kodansha America, Inc.

Library of Congress Cataloging-in-Publication Data

Thompson, Helen, 1948–
   In celebration of winter: a book of seasonal indulgences/Helen
Thompson
      p. cm.
   ISBN 1-56836-191-2 (alk. paper)
    1. Handicraft. 2. Cookery. 3. Winter—Miscellanea. I. Title.
  TT157.T51525 1997
  745.5—dc21   97-3604

In Celebration of Winter is produced by becker&mayer!, Ltd.
Book design by Heidi Baughman
Cover illustration by Kristin Knutson
Interior illustrations by Carolyn Vibbert
Edited by Jennifer Worick

Manufactured in Singapore on acid-free paper

97 98 99 00   10 9 8 7 6 5 4 3 2 1

Contents

Make a Birdfeeder from Pinecones

OST OF NATURE lies low in the winter—plants spread their regenerating roots underground, pets look for a cozy corner on the bed, and some birds—the pigeon, the cardinal, the red-crowned Cassin's finch—hunker down in readiness for the cold weather. Even the birds that do migrate stop to feed or rest in trees, along the shore, in marshes, in parks, and at bird feeders in backyards. Whether the birds are on their arduous journey south or seeking shelter from the cold, food is scarcer, so indulge them by making a special feeder for them.

Project

WINTER BIRD FEEDER

    2 pinecones
    florist's wire
    1 cup lard (no substitutes!)
    1 cup crunchy peanut butter
    2 cups quick-cook oatmeal
    1 cup white flour
    ⅓ cup sugar
    2 cups birdseed

Attach the wire to the top of the pinecones so that you can hang them from low branches.

Melt the lard and peanut butter together. Stir in the flour and sugar, and spread the mixture generously over the pinecones. Spread the birdseed onto newspaper on a flat surface, then roll the pinecones in the birdseed. Hang the cones on branches near a window, and watch birds of all kinds enjoy their high-energy treat.

    Makes 2 pinecones

OU PROBABLY ASSOCIATE picnics with summertime, but you can actually enjoy them year-round if the weather permits. And if your favorite time of year is winter, there's no reason why you can't have a picnic in the snow. This outdoor repast works especially well if you combine it with exercise (ice-skating, cross-country skiing, snowshoeing, even a good hike) to keep you warm and make you hungry for a hearty alfresco meal. You can even spread a blanket on the ground: use one that's thermal and moisture-resistant, or put a plastic trash bag on the ground first, then place the blanket over it. Use plastic plates, a wide-mouthed thermos to keep soup steaming hot, and insulated containers to make sure the sandwiches stay warm and dry.

No picnic, even a winter one, is complete without potato salad—but when it's cold, try a warm potato salad. It's a delicious accompaniment to a hearty bowl of clam and oyster bisque.

Projects

WARM POTATO SALAD

> 2 pounds small to medium-size new potatoes, halved
>   and quartered
> 1/2 cup dry white wine
> 1 bunch scallions, trimmed and thinly sliced
> 1/4 cup extra-virgin olive oil
> salt and pepper to taste

Cook the potatoes in boiling salted water until tender (about 15 minutes). Drain them in a colander.

Transfer the potatoes to a bowl, and pour the wine over them. Toss and blend.

Add the scallions, oil, salt, and pepper, and toss. Serve warm.

Serves 4

CLAM AND OYSTER BISQUE

1½ sticks butter
2 small onions, finely chopped
1 stalk celery, finely chopped
4 sprigs parsley, finely chopped
24 fresh clams, shelled and chopped
24 fresh oysters, shucked and chopped
7 cups half-and-half
salt and pepper to taste

Heat 3 tablespoons of the butter in a large saucepan, add the onion, celery, and parsley, and sauté over low heat for 2 minutes. Add 3 more tablespoons of the butter and the clams and oysters, sauté for 5 more minutes, stirring, and transfer the mixture to a blender or food processor. Add the half-and-half, purée the mixture, pour the soup back into the pan, and bring almost to a boil. Add the salt, pepper, and remaining butter, and blend well, stirring over the heat. Pour into a thermos and enjoy!

Serves 4

ANY OF LIFE'S LANDMARKS are measured and remembered in winter: a married couple's first Christmas, a baby's first tree, the year the snow was too deep to travel. Christmas ornaments are vivid mementos of the holidays, but they also offer insights into personal histories. Everyone had their favorites, of course. Maybe yours was a glittering glass globe, or a gilded fruit, or a little wooden angel with gossamer gold ringlets. Or maybe it was the star you always put on top of the tree first, before any other ornament. You may have liked the tiny white lights that nestled like stars in the tree's branches the best—or the drama of blazing Technicolor and tinsel.

ORNAMENT BOWLS

Fill bowls and baskets with ornaments, old and new, as sentimental reminders of Christmases past, and the bright hope of
all those to come.

AKING VISITORS FEEL WELCOME by preparing your guest room especially for them is one of the great pleasures of the holiday season. If your guest is a relative, set out a long-unseen family heirloom, or perhaps a photo album that will spark childhood memories. Likewise, a nonsensical toy or a favorite midnight snack on the dresser will convey your excitement at a friend's arrival. Small gestures are an important part of being a gracious host: a posy on the pillow or a decanter by the bed will let your guests know that you appreciate them and that, for the duration of their stay, your house is their haven.

Project

PREP A GUEST ROOM

Get ready for holiday guests by outfitting your guest room
with a good armchair, a reading light, books and magazines
for late-night browsing, soft blankets, fresh potpourri, a night-
light, a terry robe and slippers, fresh glycerin soap, an extra
toothbrush, and, on the day of arrival, a nosegay on the bedside. Then indulge yourself by testing out the room a few
days before your guests arrive.

Roast a Goose

HE TRADITIONAL ROAST TURKEY or goose was one of the culinary high points of Christmas Day, so eagerly anticipated that it seemed that dinner would never come. Who hasn't sneaked a morsel of crisp skin off the turkey when no one was looking? Or deftly dipped a finger into a bowl of dressing? Directions for roasting a goose follow a general standard; recipes for stuffing probably vary more than for any other dish. One old farm rule always applies, though: you need one cup of stuffing for every pound of bird.

Remember, the safe time to stuff poultry is just before you put it in the oven. After dinner, remove the stuffing at once, and refrigerate.

Project

CHRISTMAS GOOSE WITH FRUIT STUFFING

> *ready-to-cook goose with giblets*
>
> *1 quart water*
>
> *2 (8-ounce) packages of herb-seasoned stuffing*
>
> *2 cups fresh cranberries, washed and mashed*
>
> *¼ pound fresh mushrooms, wiped and chopped*
>
> *1 (1-pound) can sweetened plums, drained, pitted, and*
> *quartered (reserve ½ cup of juice)*
>
> *1 tablespoon salt*
>
> *¼ teaspoon freshly ground pepper*

Because a young goose is tender, it cooks more quickly than a mature goose. Allow from 1 to 1½ pounds of uncooked weight per person.

Simmer the giblets in water until tender (about 1 hour). Reserve ½ cup of the cooking broth from the giblets. Chop the giblets into fine pieces.

Mix the prepared poultry stuffing, cranberries, mushrooms, plums, and ½ cup plum juice, salt, pepper, chopped giblets, and ½ cup giblet broth.

Fill the neck and body cavities with the stuffing.

Place the goose breast-side down on the rack in a large roasting pan. Roast uncovered in the oven at 325 degrees F for 3 to 4 hours (about 20 minutes per pound). Turn the bird breast-side up about two-thirds of the way through the roasting time. During roasting, spoon or siphon off fat as it accumulates in the pan.

Test for doneness by moving the drumstick up and down. The joints should yield readily, and the meat should feel soft. Do not undercook the goose.

Give Champagne to the Hostess or Host

RING CHAMPAGNE to a holiday party as a gift for your host—it's a glamorous present and gives the impression of being far more extravagant than it really is. The very uncorking of the bottle is festive, and no important occasion is quite complete without it. High society has enjoyed the sparkling effervescence of this wine ever since Dom Perignon pioneered the champagne-making process in 1698. In America, champagne even dodged Prohibition: the affluent and privileged could still indulge at swank watering holes like the Stork Club and El Morocco—and an entire generation of songsters, including Cole Porter and George Gershwin, paid tribute to its heady powers.

CHAMPAGNE COCKTAIL: THE MOSCOW MULE

ice

vodka

champagne, ginger beer, or ginger ale

fresh limes

fresh cucumber (optional)

Fill a copper mug with ice. Combine a shot of vodka and juice from ½ a lime, and pour over the ice in the mug. Fill the mug with champagne, ginger beer, or ginger ale. Garnish with a slice of cucumber or a wedge of lime. Pour over ice.

O FABRIC CAPTURES the moody magic of winter like velvet. This season, find a place for this sumptuous fabric somewhere in your house: draped over a daybed, framing windows, or covering a chair. Despite its disarming richness, velvet is a sturdy fabric that has actually done duty as early theater seating and car upholstery; during Marie Antoinette's time, wool velvet was even used as a floor covering (the precursor to wall-to-wall carpeting). So a wintertime splurge on this luxurious fabric really makes sense—you can't have too much of it.

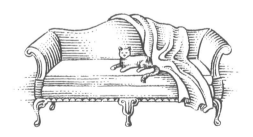

Projects

VELVET BEDCOVER

For an opulent winter bedspread, splurge on velvet from your local fabric store. Using a tape measure, take measurements starting at the floor on each side of your bed. Add 6 inches to allow for the hem. Hem the edges with a machine stitch or by hand, and back with a cool linen, brocade, or satin. The cover's magnificent texture will make you feel positively regal. Coordinate a lampshade with the other colors in your room by gluing a velvet ribbon around its top and bottom edges.

VELVET SCARF

2 yards velvet
2 yards silk, velvet, or synthetic fabric in contrasting colors
cotton thread in matching or contrasting colors
scissors

Wrap yourself in luxury with a velvet scarf. Cut the fabric 1½ to 2 yards long and 16 inches wide. As backing, use silk, velvet, or a synthetic fabric in the same dimensions. Place the right sides of the fabrics together, and stitch a ½-inch seam around the edges, leaving 12 inches open on one long side. Clip each corner on the diagonal, and turn the scarf right-side out. Hand-stitch the opening.

AGOOD FIRE CREATES a feeling of contentment as much as it does warmth. You have only to think back to the campfires of your youth to recall that a crackling fire was an essential, and hypnotic, contributor to conviviality. And even if the night was black and forbidding, a fire made you feel safe. People love to gather round a fire—whether it's a humble campfire, a roaring bonfire, or a cozy fire in your own fireplace—and building one can add ambiance to a social occasion.

Project

BUILD A PROPER FIRE

First, crumple sheets of newspaper into grapefruit-size balls or twist them into batons, and place them in the fireplace. Crisscross pieces of wood tinder (fine, feathery dead pine branch tips work best) and kindling (sticks and branches) above and around the newspaper in a square or triangular shape. Then place the larger kindling on top. (To add fragrance to the fire, make a small mound of citrus rinds under the large kindling.) Lay a few thin split logs over the tinder and kindling (and citrus rinds), leaving at least 1 inch of space in between. Light the fire now (ordinary wooden kitchen matches work best). As the fire begins to catch and blaze, add more logs, being careful not to overfeed. Finally, let the fire do the rest of the work; it should roar happily all evening. Add more logs—you shouldn't need more kindling—when the flames begin to dwindle. Adjust logs with a poker until the flame catches.

Make a Stocking

I F THERE IS A SINGLE item that epitomizes holiday gift-giving, it is the Christmas stocking, which once a year comes out of retirement and assumes its rightful place on the mantel. A cornucopia of little gifts and surprises, it is usually the first thing sought in the thrilling darkness of Christmas morning. If a loved one has worn out a stocking from many Christmases of wear and tear or was never fortunate enough to have one—make a new stocking for the deprived individual. Or if there's a new baby in the family, make the baby's first stocking; it may last a lifetime, but even if it doesn't, the child will remember it forever.

Project

MAKE A CHRISTMAS STOCKING

> *felt or another fabric of choice such as organza, brocade,*
> *or satin (½ yard for stocking, ⅛ yard for cuff)*
> *adorments such as rhinestones, sequins, buttons, jewels,*
> *bells, fringe, or ribbon*
> *glue*

Felt is a traditional material for stockings; it is easy to cut and requires no hemming. If you are stitching a design or applying buttons, jewels, sequins, or cutouts, remember to sew them on before you sew each side of the stocking together. Gluing rhinestones or cut-out felt patterns, such as bells or Christmas trees, also works well with felt. The results, however, won't be as long-lasting.

Velvets, brocades, satins, and even seductively sheer organzas also make wonderful stockings. Look for sumptuous fabrics on the remnant counters of fabric stores or upholstery shops. Antique shops and vintage stores are also good sources for fabrics.

Trace your pattern on a sheet of heavy paper, and then pin it to the fabric. Cut out the design for front and back, making sure that the stocking is big enough at the toe so that a hand can reach into it comfortably. Allow extra material at the top if you are adding a cuff to the top of the stocking.

Attach a length of satin or metallic ribbon at the top corner for hanging.

Trim with bells, buttons, fringe, silk flowers, rhinestones, or anything that reminds you of the holidays.

Force Bulbs

FORCING BULBS FOR wintertime blooming can produce one of the best flower shows of the year. Plant lots of bulbs, staggering them so that they bloom throughout the winter. Begin with the most spectacular—and easiest—of all flowers to force, the gorgeously showy amaryllis. The paper-white narcissus, with its white-stockinged stem, is also among the first to bloom; its musky fragrance will penetrate every corner of a room. Daffodils, golden and deeply sweet-smelling, are next; crocuses, tulips, and hyacinths bloom quickly after. And last? The fragile lily of the valley, with its dainty sprays of white bell-like blossoms.

Project

FORCING BULBS

Amaryllis: The amaryllis is amazingly easy to force. Select only tip-size bulbs (28 to 34 centimeters in diameter) that force well indoors. Plant them in a 6-inch pot filled with potting soil to within 1 inch of the rim; the pot should have a drainage hole. The top half of the bulb should sit above the soil line. Water once, and then place the pot in a warm room. When signs of growth begin to appear, move the pot to your brightest window. Water and fertilize the plant.

Daffodil, tulip, and hyacinth: These are hardy bulbs that need about 6 to 10 weeks of temperatures between 35 and 45 degrees to flower; in the refrigerator or outdoors in a garage are both good spots. Then move the bulbs to a shady spot for several days, before placing them in a sunny window where the temperature should be between 50 and 65 degrees. Water the soil when it looks dry. When buds appear, move the plants to indirect light.

Freesia, crocus, and narcissus: These are tender bulbs, and should be potted in the autumn and left indoors in a cool spot (50 degrees). Keep the soil damp. When the roots start to develop (test by tugging gently on a bulb; if it resists, the roots are established), move the bulbs to a sunnier and warmer area (55 to 60 degrees). After the buds open, move them to indirect light. Rest the bulbs in dry soil in the summer.

A stunning presentation for spring bulbs is to plant them in pebbles or in water (hyacinths, crocuses, and narcissus do well in water alone). Bury the bottom of the bulb in a water-filled container of pebbles, keeping its base just above the waterline. When the shoots are several inches tall, move the container to a window.

Fertilize the bulbs after they flower if you intend to save them for replanting.

Make a Recipe from Your Childhood

OU MAY NOT BE ABLE to get away with it at other times of year, but sentimentality during the holidays is entirely appropriate. One of the ways to remember your connection to family and friends is to make a recipe that someone you care about has handed down. All the better if it's a recipe you adored as a child or one a parent used to make especially for you.

Project

SOFT MOLASSES COOKIES

1 cup butter
1 cup sugar
1 large egg
1 cup light molasses
4 ³/₄ cups sifted flour
3 teaspoons baking soda
¹/₂ teaspoon salt

1 teaspoon instant coffee
*   powder*
2 teaspoons ground cinnamon
1 teaspoon ground ginger
¹/₂ teaspoon ground cloves
³/₄ cup milk
raisins or walnut halves

Beat the butter until light. Gradually add the sugar and beat until fluffy. Beat in the egg until it is thoroughly blended, then beat in the molasses. Sift together the flour, baking soda, salt, coffee powder, and spices. Add to the molasses mixture, alternating it with the milk as you pour. Beat about 30 seconds. Drop the dough by heaping teaspoonfuls about 2 inches apart onto a lightly greased baking sheet. Try to keep the cookies round. Press a raisin or a walnut half in the center of each cookie. Bake in the oven at 375 degrees F for about 12 to 15 minutes. Place the cookies on racks to cool.

Makes about 5 dozen cookies

OR CENTURIES, flowers were considered essential for running a household. They were crystallized for decoration and as sweetmeats, and made into syrups, conserves, jellies, jams, sauces, liqueurs, wines, tarts, and custards. Fresh, they were strewn over salads, soups, and stews; dried, they were preserved as medicine or for scent during the winter.

Cooking with flowers is rewarding just because they are so beautiful and so simple to work with. One lovely and easy holiday gift is a jar of sugar, layered with flowers and citrus peels. Flower-scented sugars add fragrance to cakes, cookies, custards, whipping cream, and sweets. Choose the sweeter aromatic flowers—hyssop, lavender, lilacs, roses, scented geraniums, and sweet violets.

Project

SCENTED SUGAR

This is a simple but sweet gift that can be packaged in any kind of jar, from a homely Mason jar to one made from exotic cut glass.

> *edible flowers and leaves such as roses, geraniums,*
>   *or pansies*
> *oranges*
> *lemons*
> *granulated sugar*
> *decorative jar*

Layer granulated sugar with edible flowers, leaves, or peels (orange or lemon peel should dry for 1 day). Leave about ½ inch of headspace at the top. Put on the lid, shake the jar, and place it on a shelf in a cool, dark place for 2 or 3 weeks. The sugar will become more intensely fragrant with age.

Make a Sweet Dreams Pillow from Rosemary

INTER IS A GOOD TIME to appreciate rosemary, one of nature's hardiest plants. The diminutive woody herb with pinelike needles makes a gloriously pungent display indoors in pots placed on a tray of pebbles for good drainage. Set the tray near a window, and enjoy the midwinter greenery as an aromatic; as a garnish for fish, poultry, and meats; and as a restorative known for calming headaches, indigestion, depression, muscle pain, and insomnia.

Project

ROSEMARY SLEEP PILLOW

> *lacy handkerchief*
> *thread*
> *muslin, tulle, or thin fabric the same size as your handkerchiefs*
> *mortar and pestle*
> *fresh rosemary*
> *glycerin or alcohol*
> *other dried flowers and herbs (optional)*

To make a rosemary sleep pillow, first fashion a dainty envelope from a lacy hanky by sewing two sides together, leaving enough material at the top to fold over for the outer pillow. For the inner herb bag, make a smaller version in muslin, tulle, or other thin fabric. Gently crush a handful of fresh rosemary with a mortar and pestle or by hand, making sure no sharp or tough parts remain. Sprinkle the crushed rosemary with water and a trace of alcohol or glycerin, and place in the herb bag. You can also add dried flowers and other herbs—such as rose petals, sage, lavender, or eucalyptus—from your favorite herb shop. Baste the muslin inner envelope closed, place it inside the hanky envelope, then tuck it inside your pillow case or under your pillow.

Send Yourself a Bouquet

ENDING A BOUQUET of flowers is usually a gesture reserved for special occasions such as Valentine's Day, Mother's Day, or a birthday. This year, why not purchase a three- or six-month flower delivery service just for yourself? It's an extravagance, but one you certainly deserve. Reward yourself for dealing with a difficult task this year, or for completing a job particularly well. Or just order flowers to ward off the midwinter blues. You can either opt for merry seasonal arrangements to commemorate the holidays, or for exotic tropicals (such as the vivid bird-of-paradise) to take your mind off the weather. Either way, it will be a pleasant surprise each time the delivery arrives.

Make Sugared or Gilded Fruits

I N WINTER, when flowers and fruit are traditionally at their scarcest, you might think of preserving them with sugar, or more permanently with gilt wax polish. This old-style practice produces frosty fruit sculptures that make lavish centerpieces or mantel displays. For sugared fruits, use fresh fruits of varying sizes and shapes, but remember that smooth-skinned fruits work best. For polishing, a wider variety of choices is available— old oranges, lemons, limes, seed cases, nut pods, pinecones, leaves, gourds, thistles, and nuts all offer vivid contrast. Sugared and gilded fruits should last a few months.

Projects

SUGARED FRUIT

Sugared pears, grapes, plums, and apples will glisten delicately grouped in a bowl or piled high on a mantel.

variety of fruits
2 egg whites for each fruit
crystallized or colored sugars

Dip the fruit in egg whites. Roll it in crystallized sugar or, for a Technicolor effect, use colored sugars. Let dry completely. Arrange the fruit in a glass bowl.

GILDED FRUIT

Polishing fruit with gilt wax is the proper way to achieve a lustrous silvered effect (replicating this look with silver spray paint is messier and tends to produce a garish look).

jar of silver gilt wax
fine watercolor brush
clean shoe brush or a soft cloth

Twist the watercolor brush around in the jar of wax until it is covered with wax. Lightly brush your botanicals and fruit. Polish to the desired luster with a shoe brush or soft cloth. Arrange in a basket, filling in the gaps with dried roses or other dried flowers, or with green moss.

Host a New Year's Day Brunch

HERE IS SOMETHING very indulgent about a late breakfast, especially after a long night of party-ing. To round out the holiday season, why not treat your friends to a New Year's Day brunch? Most people don't *give* parties on January 1, but they really need to go to one. Make this occasion merry but restorative, and serve nourishing, wholesome food. If ever there was a time for comfort food, New Year's Day is it.

Projects

SPICED CRANBERRY NECTAR

Make the spiced cranberry syrup ahead of time and then
refrigerate it.

 3½ cups sugar

 6 cups cold water

 2 lemons

 3 pounds cranberries

 8 slices fresh ginger

 3 cinnamon sticks

Combine the sugar with the water in a large saucepan,
and cook over medium heat, stirring until the sugar has
dissolved. Squeeze the juice from the lemons, reserving the
rinds. Add the juice and rinds to the syrup, along with the
cranberries, ginger, and cinnamon sticks. Bring to a boil,
reduce the heat to low, and cook uncovered until most of
the berries pop (10 to 15 minutes), skimming the froth off
the surface. Remove from the heat and let stand for ½ hour.
Strain the syrup through a fine sieve, pressing down on
the berries to release as much juice as possible. Cover
and refrigerate.

For the nectar, you will need:

6 cups spiced cranberry syrup

6 cups fresh orange juice

ice cubes

seltzer or soda water

6 orange slices, halved

Stir the cranberry syrup and orange juice in a large pitcher. Place the ice cubes in tall tumblers. Pour in the cranberry-orange mixture, and add a splash of seltzer or soda. Garnish with orange slices, and serve.

Makes 8 cups

BUTTERMILK BISCUITS

1 cup all-purpose flour

1 cup whole wheat flour

1 teaspoon baking powder

¼ teaspoon baking soda

1 teaspoon salt

¼ cup vegetable shortening

¾ cup buttermilk

Preheat the oven to 400 degrees F.

Using a whisk, stir together the flours and the baking powder, baking soda, and salt in a large bowl. Cut the shortening into the flour with two knives, using a scissors-like motion, until the mixture has the consistency of cornmeal. Stir in the buttermilk (don't worry if the flour isn't completely incorporated into the mixture). Turn the dough and any flour remaining in the bowl out onto a lightly floured surface and knead 12 times. Roll into a 10-inch circle, ½ inch thick. Cut into 2-inch-diameter circles using a cookie cutter or a knife, and place the biscuits on an ungreased baking sheet. Bake for 15 minutes or until golden brown. Serve with real butter, or garnish with fruit jam.

Makes 15 biscuits

Make Spice Balls from Oranges and Lemons

RUIT AND SPICES work magic on your senses, especially in winter, and bold and sunny oranges are particularly effective antidotes to seasonal melancholy. In the Middle Ages homes were scented with clove oranges, a tangy combination that was aromatic as well as eye-catching. Decorate a dozen or so oranges with cloves, varying the patterns—and don't forget to include lemons and limes, too.

Project

SPICE BALLS

    oranges, lemons, limes

    cloves

    darning needle or fine skewer

    cinnamon

    orrisroot

    cinnamon sticks

    Stud each fruit with cloves. If the rind is tough, pierce your pattern first with the darning needle or skewer. Use a solid overall pattern, a curving concentric circle pattern, or create one that is uniquely your own. Then for fragrance roll the studded oranges in cinnamon and orrisroot (a preservative). Display in bowls along with cinnamon sticks tied with ribbon.

ECORATING A HOUSE with garlands and wreaths is an ancient custom, and it always creates a festive air you wish you could maintain all year long.

Holiday wreaths are easy enough to buy—and there are thousands to choose from—but they are also easy to make. And you can be sure that your wreath will look just the way you want it to and match your holiday mood exactly.

Fir boughs are wonderfully evocative of the season and smell good, too, but take advantage of other natural bounty such as pink pepper berries, pinecones, moss, eucalyptus, acorns, birds' nests, and even dried flowers. And if nature doesn't quite provide the sense of drama you're striving for, try a delicate wire wreath entwined with strings of crystals, colored stones, and pearls.

Project

MOSS WREATH

> *Styrofoam, wire, or straw frame*
> *moss, bird's nests, twigs, acorns*
> *hot glue gun*
> *florist's wire*
> *leaves or flowers as desired*
> *silica gel if necessary*

To make a simple moss wreath, or even one that is heavily embellished, use a Styrofoam or straw frame and attach moss, birds' nests, twigs, and acorns with a hot-glue gun. Eucalyptus, pepper berry, or pinecone wreaths look prettier made from vine wreaths (let the vine show through). Attach the berries and leaves with florist's wire. To make a flower wreath—daffodils, roses, lilacs, viburnums, and hydrangeas are perfect—buy or cut the flowers fresh, and preserve them in 1 inch of silica gel for a day. Using a wire wreath form, apply dry sheet moss first with the hot-glue gun. Then place the larger blooms on the moss, one section at a time. Fill in with smaller blooms. This wreath looks best densely packed with flowers.

Make Cookie Gift Tags

HERE'S MORE TO GIVING a gift than just picking it out. The time you spend thinking about it and the way you present it also make it special. The tag you choose to announce your gift should be just as singular as the gift itself—so garnish your presents this holiday with ornaments, perhaps a watercolor tag you've painted, an old snapshot, a piece of jewelry, or even a cookie personalized with the recipient's initial and embellished with a flourish of ribbon.

Project

GINGERBREAD COOKIE GIFT TAGS

> 2 sticks unsalted butter
>
> 1 cup packed dark brown sugar
>
> 4 teaspoons ground ginger
>
> 4 teaspoons cinnamon
>
> $1\frac{1}{2}$ teaspoons ground cloves
>
> 1 teaspoon finely ground black pepper
>
> 2 teaspoons baking soda
>
> $1\frac{1}{2}$ teaspoons salt
>
> 2 large eggs
>
> $\frac{3}{4}$ cup plus 2 tablespoons dark molasses
>
> 6 cups all-purpose flour

Cream the butter and sugar with the paddle attachment in an electric mixer, until fluffy. Mix in the ginger, cinnamon, cloves, pepper, baking soda, and salt. Beat in the eggs and molasses.

Add the flour and mix on low speed. Divide the dough into thirds, and press to flatten. Wrap in plastic. Chill in the refrigerator for at least 1 hour.

Heat the oven to 350 degrees F. Flour two pieces of parchment. Roll out each piece of dough on the parchment until it is ⅛-inch thick. Cover with another sheet of parchment, and place in the freezer for 15 minutes.

Remove from the freezer. Using cookie cutters of your choice, begin cutting. You can use alphabet cookie cutters, or emboss cookies with initials using a smaller alphabet cookie cutter. Transfer the cookies to a parchment-lined baking sheet. Make a ⅛-inch hole for the ribbon, using a round pastry tip. Cover the cookies with parchment. Place a second cookie sheet on top to keep them flat while baking.

Bake about 35 minutes or until the cookies are lightly browned. Remove and transfer them to a wire rack; do not remove the top cookie sheet until the cookies are cool.

Makes 30 cookies

Make Real Hot Chocolate

A STEAMING CUP of hot chocolate is perfect in cold weather: not only does it smell and taste wonderful, it will warm your hands and face. It was the Aztecs, in fact, who first harvested the cacao bean and made cocoa drinks flavored with vanilla and spices. Later, the Europeans considered chocolate to be one of the finer things in life, and it was so expensive that only the wealthy could afford it. Even today, good chocolate is still a treat—everyday consumption would be excessive, if not extravagant. But there are times, such as quiet evenings at home, when you should treat yourself and your friends. Making real hot chocolate requires only a little more time than using a prepared mix, and it is delicious.

Project

REAL HOT COCOA

> 10 tablespoons unsweetened cocoa
>
> ½ cup sugar
>
> ½ cup water
>
> 4 cups milk
>
> 4 cups half-and-half

Combine the cocoa, sugar, and water in a large saucepan and bring to a boil, then lower the heat, and simmer for 2 or 3 minutes. Gradually add the milk, stirring constantly. Then gradually stir in the half-and-half. Bring just to a boil, and remove from the heat. Pour the chocolate into mugs immediately and garnish with a dollop of whipped cream, cinnamon, or cinnamon sticks.

Makes 6 servings

THIS IS THE SEASON you stop and take stock of what's really important in life. Your thoughts may even turn to that family holiday gathering you never made, or a favorite relative who is no longer alive, or a friend you seldom see. Perhaps the best gift you could give this year is to track down a lost friend. The search might prove to be as much fun as finding the person, for you might end up reestablishing other neglected friendships along the way.

POTATO-PRINT STATIONERY OR HOLIDAY CARDS

When writing to inquire about your friend's whereabouts, use hand-designed stationery to personalize your efforts. In fact, you can create impressionistic designs with very little effort.

> *potato*
> *pencil*
> *X-acto knife*
> *gouache paints*
> *brush*
> *paper or cards, any kind*

Cut a potato in half, and draw a shape onto the flesh with a pencil. With an X-acto knife or a small carving knife, carve around the outline and cut away either the background or the penciled design to a depth of ¼ inch. Mix gouache paints (available from an art supply store) with a little water, and apply to the design with a brush; you can also dip the potato directly into a dish containing the paint. Press the potato onto the paper (any kind of paper will work, but recycled paper or paper with a pronounced grain will look best). To make a card, fold the paper in half, with the potato print on the front, and write your greeting inside.

OU'RE BOUND TO FIND a permanent spot in your house for these decorative stacking boxes, even without gifts inside them. Use one for a single dramatic presentation, or several stacked on top of one another as a sequential gift, or simply as pretty packages in their own right that will make wonderful hideaways for secret trinkets and valued treasures.

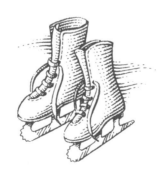

Project

STACKING BOXES

> *lidded boxes (available at craft stores)*
> *sateen, raw silk, velvet, brocade, linen, ultra suede*
>   *(amount needed depends on the size of the box)*
> *fusible web*
> *⅜-inch twisted cording*
> *tassel*
> *hot-glue gun*
> *iron*

You will need to purchase the boxes from a craft shop first in order to determine the answer of fabric required.

Center the bottom of the box on the wrong side of the fabric, and fold and cut the fabric to the same dimensions on all sides of the box, leaving an extra inch all around. Cut a piece of fabric to fit the inside bottom of the box, adding ½ inch all around. Fold and cut a piece of fabric to the same dimensions as the box lid, adding 1 inch all around. Cut a piece of fabric to fit inside the top of the lid, adding ½ inch all around. With a hot iron, fuse the fusible web to the wrong side of the fabric, following the instructions on the web packaging. Fold the fabric over the right side of the box, with the raw edges to the wrong side, and fuse in place. Fold the edges to the wrong side along each edge of the bottom piece and fuse in place inside the box, covering the raw edges. In the same manner, fuse the top lid piece in place, then do the same with the inside of the lid. Arrange the twisted cording around the outside edges of the lid top. Tie the ends into a knot. Cut the excess and glue the ends with the glue gun underneath the decorative knot. Glue the tassel to the knot. Glue the twisted cording in place on the lid top.

I T CAN BE WONDERFUL to curl up in a cozy chair on a long winter evening and linger over a good book. If the book is an old favorite and has become dog-eared and tattered after years of being toted around, why not make a slipcover for it? This one comes with its own bookmark attached so that everything you'll need is right at hand. A pretty slipcover for a book also makes a delightful gift; it's one of those luxuries that most people could use, but never buy for themselves. Ship a new book inside the cover, and give your favorite bookworm a double treat.

BOOK SLIPCOVER

> *flannel, brocade, suede, linen, sateen, velvet, or vintage fabric*
> *pinking shears*
> *iron*
> *needle and cotton thread*
> *ribbon*

Trim sizes for books can vary: a hardcover novel could measure $6\frac{1}{8}$ x $9\frac{1}{4}$ inches, a paperback $5\frac{1}{2}$ x $8\frac{1}{4}$ inches.

Open the book, and cut the fabric 8 inches wider and 3 inches longer than the opened book. With the fabric's wrong side up, fold the long sides $1\frac{1}{2}$ inches, and iron until the edges are smooth. Fold the short sides 1 inch and press again. Fold the short sides another 3 inches to form the flaps that will hold the book's cover, and press again. Center the book on the fabric, insert the front and back covers into the flaps, and pull the fabric taut—this will determine whether the slipcover is the correct size. Make a bookmark by sewing in the piece of ribbon to the top middle of the slipcover. Finally, sew the cover flaps closed by hand at the top and bottom, using a slip stitch.

Make a Christmas Tree Out of Old Glass Balls

F YOU'RE IN THE HABIT of packing away Christmas ornaments at the end of each holiday, you may find that some of the older ones end up farther and farther back in the closet. Go on a search for any over-looked boxes of ornaments: even if they don't have the glossy sheen of more modern decorations, they are still worth salvaging, if only for their sentimental value. Glass balls are the most humble of Christmas ornaments—remember, at one time they all came from Woolworth's, the first retailer to sell Christmas balls. A glass-ball Christmas tree can be a little monument to less-than-perfect glass globes, their aged or damaged sides hidden from view by the surrounding balls. An old garden urn will make a dramatic stand for your tree; set it on a table or console, or place two trees on either side of your fireplace.

If you're interested in this project, but don't have any old ornaments on hand, try a flea market or junk shop; glass balls commonly end up in estate sales and are easy to find.

Project

GLASS-BALL CHRISTMAS TREE

>*Styrofoam cone in height desired (bigger is better)*
>*at least 250 glass balls (for 18-inch-tall cone) from ½ inch
>   to 1½ inches in diameter, in silvers, golds, and a
>   contrasting color*
>*hot glue gun*
>*antique garden urn or decorative pot*

Start at the bottom of the cone, and glue the largest balls in place, one at a time, until the cone is completely covered with balls.

Make a Skirt for Your Christmas Tree

HRISTMAS TREE SKIRTS were invented to hide those Gothic-looking stands that never quite fit the tree. And they were useful for catching dry pine needles, thus saving a lot of cleanup when the tree was dismantled. A skirt also provided a plush setting for displaying gifts, especially if it was lavished with sequins and beads. It was as if the ornaments had actually fallen into the satin folds of the skirt, where they lay twinkling around the unopened presents. This setting was, and still is, captivating for a small child, particularly one determined to sit for hours in front of the tree speculating on the contents of all the mysterious packages. Since Christmas tree skirts are so easy to make, you should probably have several.

Project

TREE SKIRT

pencil
5 yards of string
butcher paper
5 yards of 56-inch-wide
   taffeta, brocade, satin, or
   vintage fabric
scissors

needle and thread
felt
hook-and-eye closures
fringe or decorative braid
decorative beads, sequins, or
   buttons

Using your pencil as a compass, tie the string to the tip and make a large circle on butcher paper, holding the other end of the string in one place at the center of the paper. Make a smaller circle in the center to accommodate the tree trunk. Cut one large circle out of the taffeta (or other fabric) and one out of the felt. Cut the center hole out of each piece of fabric, and cut along the radius (one straight cut from the center to the edge) so that the skirt can wrap around the trunk. Hem the bottom, edges, and center hole of the taffeta skirt. Baste the taffeta, right-side up, and felt pieces together at the center hole and along the two straight edges. Add hook-and-eye closures to the radius cut. Sew on a fringe or braid around the hem, then decorate the skirt with beads, sequins, or buttons.

F IT'S TOO BITTER to go out, it may be a good time to refurbish those summer flea market finds. A battered table with a scarred top is just the right surface for a mosaic, either free-form or a copy of a classic pattern. Using colored stones, glass, mirror shards, tile, even rocks, you can create your own version of a mosaic—and cover almost anything from vases and frames to floors and walls.

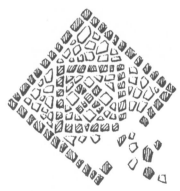

MOSAIC TABLE

> *pencil*
>
> *paper*
>
> *tesserae: glazed ceramic, opaque glass and porcelain tiles,*
>   *and broken stained or mirror glass (most mosaic tiles can*
>   *be purchased pre-cut at a craft store; found shards work*
>   *equally well)*
>
> *tile nippers (wear protective glasses when cutting)*
>
> *tweezers*
>
> *white glue*
>
> *grout*
>
> *rubber spatula*
>
> *sponge*
>
> *molding (optional)*
>
> *stiff-bristled scrub brush*
>
> *liquid floor wax*

Find a design you like, and draw its outline full-size on a
piece of paper. Cut the tiles and fit them into place on the design
so that you can judge the spacing as well as the aesthetic effect.
Play with the tesserae and the spaces between them to create the
most pleasing effect. For more detail in your mosaic, use smaller

tesserae of varying shapes. Copy your design onto the surface that you plan to tile. Apply the adhesive to the surface, and set the tiles in place. Let the glue dry overnight. The next day, mix grout in a bowl until it has the consistency of sour cream. Spread it generously over the entire surface of your mosaic with a rubber spatula, forcing grout into the spaces between the tiles. Wipe off the excess with the spatula, and clean the surface of the mosaic with a damp sponge. If you are adding molding to the edges of your table for a more finished look, nail it on now. Let the grout dry overnight. The next day, apply a second coat of grout, and rub it in between the tiles. Scrape off the excess with the spatula, and sponge the surface clean. Again, let it dry overnight. Brush the mosaic briskly with a stiff-bristled brush to smooth out the grout. Sponge the surface clean, and apply a coat of liquid floor wax to both the mosaic and the wood.

MAKING GUESTS FEEL welcome can be the most important—and often the least expensive—part of getting ready for the holidays. Little gestures count more than almost anything money can buy: turning down the bed sheets, placing a posy on a bedside table, stacking books by your guest's favorite author under a reading lamp. Stocking your guest bathroom with handmade soap will also let visitors know you think they are special. You can easily make soap without tallow, lye, soap molds, or a two-week wait for the soap to cure—and the results will reward you and your guest with festive balls of speckled and fragrant soap that are as good for giving as they are for keeping.

Project

HERBAL SOAP

  bars of Ivory soap
  knife
  cutting board
  handheld cheese grater (preferably the cylindrical kind,
      such as a Mouli)
  measuring cup
  plastic microwave bowl and plate
  lemon
  vegetable peeler
  fork
  food coloring
  measuring spoons
  minced fresh herbs such as rosemary or lavender
  microwave oven
  eyedropper
  scented oil or perfume

Cut each bar of soap into 1-inch chunks and grate into fine strings. For each soap ball, measure ½ cup of grated soap into a bowl. To add coloring or zest, peel the skin off a lemon and mince; then, with a fork, mix it into the bowl with the grated soap. Or add 2 to 5 drops of food coloring, and 1 tablespoon of minced fresh herbs such as rosemary or lavender. Microwave on high for 30 to 60 seconds or until the soap is completely foamy. Remove the soap from the oven, and turn the bowl upside down on a clean countertop. Using an eyedropper to add scent, add 10 to 20 drops of oil or perfume to the foam. Let cool only long enough so that the foam isn't too hot to handle, but work quickly while the foam is still warm. Mold the soap into a golf ball-size shape by compacting evenly on all sides between your palms, being careful not to knead the foam (this will cause cracking). Let the soap cool for 3 to 5 minutes, and then smooth and shine the surface by rolling the ball on a dinner plate.

Make a Valentine Lampshade

ONE WAY TO KEEP your love shining brightly on Valentine's Day is to inscribe a favorite message, thought, or poem on a plain white lampshade for a pretty boudoir lamp. Every time you turn on the light, your sentiments will glow as warmly as your love. This is also a sweet gift for a child who will find the lamp and its message a source of comfort and companionship throughout the night.

Project

MAKE A LAMPSHADE

    plain white lampshade

    tissue paper

    your favorite love poem or collection of sayings

    permanent fabric marker in black, red, or gold

    ¼-inch satin ribbon in coordinating color

    glue gun

Study the lamp shade before writing on it, in order to determine whether you wish to write on the diagonal, at random, or lengthwise around the shade. Stuff the inside of the shade with tissue paper to create a sturdy surface on which to write. Then lean the shade on your knee as you write, being careful not to let the tip of the fabric marker rest on the lampshade as you write (this will prevent blotching). Measure the ribbon for the top and bottom of the shade; cut and glue it on to finish.

Draw an Herbal Bath

OTHING WILL TAKE the chill out of your bones like a steamy, fragrant bath. As the ancients knew, certain aromas have curative and restorative powers. Make your own bath essence by combining oils in a bottle, preferably a dark-colored one to keep the scents from being altered by light. Or keep each oil in its own pretty bottle and line up the bottles by your bathtub so that you can combine your own fresh bath essences every day.

Project

HERBAL BATH OIL

> *10 ounces oil of violet*
> *10 ounces oil of rosemary*
> *10 ounces oil of verbena*
> *10 ounces oil of rose geranium*

Draw a hot bath. Just before turning off the tap, swirl in 12 drops of oil of violet, 6 drops of rosemary, 6 drops of verbena, and 6 drops of rose geranium. Mix gently with your fingertips.

Make a Rose Petal Frame for Your Valentine

 BOUQUET OF ROSES seems to be the universal token of love on Valentine's Day. If you feel a bouquet is too predictable, but you would still like to give flowers, try layering a picture frame with dried rose petals. Remember, always dry more petals than you think you'll need. Experiment with the colors, too: the effect of solid-color roses on a frame is slightly impressionistic, while variegated colors or light-colored petals with darker borders will create a more pronounced, scalloped pattern.

Project

ROSE PETAL FRAME

    1 dozen miniature roses such as sweetheart or porcelina
    3 pounds silica gel crystals
    airtight lidded box
    soup spoon
    spatula
    sieve
    kraft paper
    6- x 6-inch light-colored wood frame
    fine sandpaper
    paper plates
    glue (test your brands; some will turn petals a yellowish tint)
    soft, round brush (available at craft stores)
    tweezers
    burnisher
    paper towels
    waxed paper
    4-inch-wide acrylic brayer (a roller)
    8-ounce bottle acrylic matte medium

To dry petals: Peel off the petals gently, one by one. Discard the bruised ones. Pour a thin, even layer of silica gel crystals into the bottom of a box. Lay the petals in a row on the crystals, making sure they do not overlap. Sprinkle the crystals over the petals with a soup spoon until they are covered. Repeat with another layer of petals. Cover the box so that it is airtight, and set aside for 3 days. You will need approximately 95 petals for a 6- x 6-inch frame.

After 3 days, test the petals to see if they are dry. If they are still pliable, re-cover the box for another day. Once the petals feel dry to the touch, lift them from the crystals with a spatula, transfer to a sieve, and gently shake the crystals loose. Place the petals on a flat surface, arranging them by size.

To make frame: Cover the work surface with brown kraft paper, and lightly sand the frame. Pour a 3-inch-wide pool of glue on a paper plate, and select ten of the smallest petals. Place them in the glue and coat them lightly on both sides, using a round brush. Let the petals remain in the glue for about 5 minutes or until they are pliable. As you prepare to transfer the petals with tweezers to a clean area of the plate, arrange another group of petals in the glue (repeat this until your frame is completed). Transfer the petals and wipe off the excess glue with a brush; pick up each petal with tweezers and position it on the frame, the inner side of petal face up. Start applying the smallest petals to the frame's inner and outer edges first. Lay the top third of each petal on front inner edge of frame and wrap the other two-thirds around to the back of frame. Repeat. Smooth with a burnisher. Use your fingertips or a towel to wipe off the excess glue. Lay the waxed paper over the glued frame, and roll with the brayer to eliminate air bubbles. Cover the outer portion of the frame with the large petals, and work toward the inner edge using ever smaller petals. After the glue is dry, place another piece of waxed paper over the frame with a heavy book on top overnight. The next day, coat the frame lightly with acrylic matte medium to seal the petals.

ART OF THE DRAMA of Christmas springs from the mystery of the wrapped gift. There was a time when Christmas presents were laid unwrapped under a tree or stuffed in a stocking. In fact, wrapping can be as enticing as the gift itself, and can even hint at the secret inside, so choosing the right wrapping paper is important. It can also be expensive. But you can make your own signature wrapping inexpensively with brown kraft paper (similar to but thinner than the brown paper used for grocery bags), which comes wide enough to cover even the biggest present. Its plainness is a bonus because it actually enhances other colors such as gold, and provides the perfect backdrop for a variety of decorative flourishes. Use a lighter-weight kraft paper, not the heavy-weight paper used for shipping boxes.

Project

CUSTOM GIFT WRAP

lightweight brown kraft paper

French wire ribbon in desired colors, such as burgundy
  velvet or silk ribbon

gold silk cording, gold or velvet leaves (available at a craft store)

gold oil-based stamp pad paint

Fortuny pleats: Place the paper on a flat surface, and fold
into pleats about ¾ inch wide. Then, to create wrinkles along
the surface of the pleats, squeeze the stack of pleats into a ball.
Open the stack of pleats gently. Wrap your package, long sides
first. Dress with a gold or burgundy French wire ribbon.

Wrinkled wrapping: Squeeze a sheet of paper into a ball,
then open gently and smooth out the wrinkles. Repeat. Wrap
your present loosely but define its shape by creasing the wrapping along the edges. Tie with a velvet or silk ribbon and
adorn with gold or velvet leaves or berries.

Gold-speckled wrapping: Lay the sheet of brown kraft
paper on a work surface protected with newspaper. Using gold
oil-based stamp pad paint, randomly squeeze a few droplets
onto the paper. Let it dry overnight: the oil-based paint will
bleed onto the paper, forming an aura around each gold drop.
Tie the package with velvet or gold twisted cording.

Make Plum Pudding

T IS NEARLY IMPOSSIBLE to think of plum pudding without thinking of Victorian England. But it's also worth noting what the pudding actually symbolizes: its round shape represents the fertile earth; the sprig of holly with its red berries, a traditional garnish, symbolizes the blood of Christ; and the brandy flames recall the fires of the underworld that are extinguished when good triumphs over evil. The silver coins and charms (or *milagros* if you are from the Southwest or Mexico) are good luck talismans that promise happiness and prosperity in the new year.

It is a common tradition to make too much pudding, so that you can give it away during the holidays. Some cooks even insist that to make a really proper pudding, you must invite your neighbors over to stir it for good luck!

Project

PLUM PUDDING

½ cup butter

1½ cup brown sugar, firmly
    packed

2 eggs

1 teaspoon vanilla

1 cup grated and peeled
    carrots

1 cup grated and peeled tart
    apples

½ cup dark raisins

½ cup golden raisins

½ cup orange and lemon
    peel, finely chopped

½ cup currants

1 cup pecans, coarsely
    chopped

1½ cup sifted flour

¼ teaspoon cloves

1 teaspoon cinnamon

½ teaspoon ginger

½ teaspoon mace

3 tablespoons molasses

1 teaspoon baking soda

½ teaspoon salt

1 cup fresh bread crumbs

¼ pound ground beef suet

½ cup brandy or dark
Jamaican rum

silver coins or charms

holly sprigs

Cream the butter and sugar. Beat in the eggs and vanilla;
stir in the carrots, apples, raisins, citrus peel, currants, and
nuts. Sift together the flour, spices, soda, and salt, and stir into

the creamed mixture. Add the crumbs, suet, molasses, and brandy, mix well. Add the silver coins or charms. Spoon into a well-oiled 1½-quart mold. Cover the pudding securely with the mold lid or a floured, buttered, damp cloth. Place the mold on a rack in a covered pot of boiling water. The water should come halfway up on the mold. Steam for 3 hours. Unmold the pudding onto a serving plate. Serve hot with warm brandy sauce. To flame, heat 2 ounces of brandy in a small saucepan. Remove from the stove, light the brandy, and pour it—flaming—over the pudding. Carry the pudding, slowly, to the table.

Makes 8 to 10 servings

Brandy Sauce

1 large egg

1 teaspoon cornstarch

⅔ cup evaporated skim milk

⅓ cup sugar

pinch of salt

2 tablespoons brandy

In a small, heavy saucepan, whisk together the egg and cornstarch until smooth. Whisking in the evaporated skim milk, sugar, and salt over a low heat, bring the mixture to a simmer until thickened. Remove from the heat, and stir in the brandy. Let cool slightly and drizzle over the pudding.

Make Hot Buttered Cider

 ULLED CIDER is such a welcoming beverage that you should probably keep some on hand all season long as a treat for your friends and family (and yourself), especially after a day spent skiing or a night of caroling. So that you're always prepared, store the spices in a crock and keep them handy. Don't worry about proportions, because the drink will taste good, no matter what.

Project

HOT BUTTERED CIDER

Keep this fragrant spice recipe on hand for last-minute celebrations. Add to cider at preparation time.

Spice Recipe:

12 cinnamon sticks, broken in half
¼ cup whole cloves
¼ cup allspice berries

¼ cup juniper berries
1 teaspoon nutmeg
grated rinds of 2 oranges, 2 lemons, and 2 tangerines

Combine the ingredients, and store in an airtight container. To make the cider, measure a heaping teaspoon of the prepared spice mixture for each mug of cider. Simmer in a saucepan for 10 minutes. Strain and serve.

If you have the time, this from-scratch cider recipe warms and invigorates.

Cider Recipe:

1 quart water
1 cup sugar
3 tablespoons whole cloves
3 tablespoons whole allspice
2 sticks cinnamon
¼ cup crystallized ginger

6 cups apple cider
2 cups orange juice
½ cup lemon juice
1 stick butter
16 cinnamon sticks

Mix the water and sugar in a large nonaluminum saucepan. Bring to a boil, reduce the heat, and simmer 5 minutes. Remove from the heat, and stir in the cloves, allspice, cinnamon, and ginger. Let the mixture stand for at least 1 hour. Strain into a bowl, and return to the saucepan. Stir in the cider, orange juice, and lemon juice.

Serve in mugs with a slice of butter on top, and garnish with a cinnamon stick.

Makes 16 servings

LOVE CAN BE BITTERSWEET, and on Valentine's Day it may be particularly appropriate to acknowledge this with bittersweet chocolate hearts. You can make these hearts up to two weeks in advance, so if you are presenting them as a gift, you'll have the time on the day to get flowers, buy a bottle of champagne, or fix a romantic dinner for two.

This recipe for chocolate candy is easy, and it doesn't require tempering the chocolate. But if you know how to temper, go ahead and do so: the result will be glossier chocolate that doesn't need to be refrigerated.

Project

CHOCOLATE HEARTS

parchment paper

9- x 12- x 2-inch pan

pastry brush

vegetable oil

7 ounces bittersweet chocolate, coarsely chopped

stainless steel bowl

large metal offset (bent-neck) spatula

heart-shaped cookie cutter

Cut the parchment to fit the pan. Brush the pan with vegetable oil, making sure to cover the corners and center. Press the parchment onto the oiled pan, and set aside.

Place the chocolate in a medium-size stainless steel bowl. Bring a medium pot of water to a simmer and place the stainless steel bowl over, but not in, the still-simmering water. Melt the chocolate (about 4 to 6 minutes).

Remove the bowl with chocolate from the water. Dry the bottom of the bowl thoroughly (even the smallest drop of water will ruin the chocolate). Pour the chocolate into the pan. Spread the chocolate evenly and about $\frac{1}{16}$ inch thick, using the offset spatula. Freeze until the chocolate sets (about 6 minutes).

Working quickly, use the heart-shaped cookie cutter to cut out the chocolate hearts. If the chocolate begins to soften, return it briefly to the freezer. To remove the hearts from the parchment, run the spatula under them, then lay them flat in a separate container. Cover, and freeze.

For a pretty presentation, wrap each chocolate in a tinted foil and tie with a silk cord.

Makes 6 hearts

Stencil a Window

IF YOU FEEL THE VIEW from one of your windows—a small one in the bathroom or stairwell
perhaps—seems to contribute to the general
bleakness of the season, you might think of stenciling it.
Stenciling is an ancient decorative technique that requires
delicate and feathery applications of color; when applied to
glass windows, the effect can be delightfully sheer. Don't
worry about small mistakes, or drifting or bleeding paint—
they simply add to the overall charm.

Project

WINDOW STENCILS

stencils

automobile spray paint in desired colors

nontoxic particle mask

spray glue (to hold stencil in place)

newspaper (for masking areas not to be sprayed)

masking tape

cotton swabs

cotton balls

nail polish remover (to remove mistakes)

You can purchase stencils at a craft store or copy them from stencil books.

The most important thing to remember about stenciling is that you only need a little bit of paint to achieve the effect you desire, especially on a window. Use a light spray and build up the color gradually. Experiment with overlaying colors and stencils. The room should be well ventilated, but to be on the safe side, leave the room every 3 hours (although a project as simple as a small window shouldn't take that long).

Decorate Glass Ball Ornaments

FOLKTALE RELATES that when Christ was born, all the creatures on earth, including the trees, wanted to give him a present. The flowering and the fruit-bearing trees had plenty to offer, but the little fir tree only had its evergreen leaves, and so the other trees shoved it aside. Seeing its plight, an angel sent down some stars to rest in the tree's boughs, and that's how the tradition of decorating trees at Christmas began.

In fact, the tradition is not an old one. The earliest ornaments—stars, butterflies, and crosses made of lead—appeared in stores in the late nineteenth century, produced by toy makers in Nuremberg, Germany. The first hand-blown balls to be made in the United States appeared in the 1930s; mass production started in 1939. The ornaments were simple, and during the war when silvering was scarce, they became even simpler, usually clear or painted balls with stripes. You can still make your own distinctively simple ornaments in a few hours' time.

Project

GLASS BALL ORNAMENTS

Modern Striped Balls

glass ball Christmas
   ornaments
gold embossing powder
white glue
rubber bands
½-inch-wide still paintbrush
plastic drinking straws

floral foam brick
masking tape
paper towels
straight pin
tweezers
scissors
cotton swabs

Remove the cap from the ball and insert the straw into the opening. Secure the straw with tape around the opening. Clean the ball. Insert the straw and ball into the florist's foam brick. Stretch the rubber band around the circumference of the glass ornament. Add one or two other bands, if desired. Pour the embossing powder on a clean paper towel. Brush the glue over the entire surface of the ball. Holding the straw, roll the ball in the embossing powder, coating the entire surface. Replace in the foam brick and let dry for 24 hours. Then, using a straight pin, lift the rubber band, and clip with scissors. Pull off with tweezers. Replace the cap.

Star-Studded Balls

clear glass ornaments

foil stars or dots

acrylic paint in desired colors

disposable cups

wooden coffee stirrers

paper towels

glass cleaner

cotton swabs

Punch holes around the rims of the disposable cups (this will help in the drying process). Remove the cap from the ornament. Pour the paint into the ball and rotate the ball until the paint covers the entire interior surface. Pour the excess paint back into the paint container. Set the ball, open-end down, into the cup for 24 hours to dry. Clean balls, let dry, and apply the stars or dots to the surface in the desired pattern. Using the wooden coffee stirrer, burnish the stars, pressing gently from the center to the outer edges. Replace the caps.

Make a Lingerie Case

HERE ARE TWO THINGS you are likely to do during the holidays—give at least one gift and travel somewhere—and a handmade lingerie case can be a gift to yourself or to a special friend.

Project

LINGERIE ENVELOPE

> *antique lace-edged place mats or tray cloths*
> *linen fabric for the pocket*
> *matching thread*
> *pins*
> *scissors*

Cut the place mat in half across the width (A) to make the flap of the lingerie case. Cut out the linen fabric for the pocket section to match the length of one long side of the cut place mat. Be sure to allow ¾ inch on each side for the seam. Sew one long side of the cut cloth to one short side of the matching linen. Make a hem at the bottom edge of the fabric by turning back ¼ inch and then another ½ inch. Pin and machine-stitch. To complete the side seams, place the wrong sides together and fold the bottom hem up to B and pin the corners at B. Pin and then sew the two side seams (the seam allowance should be ¼ inch) using a straight stitch. Turn the case right-side out and press.

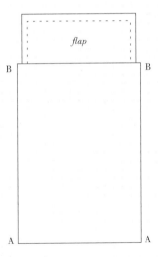

Personalize a Photo Album or Journal

HE CHRISTMAS GIFT that will make the deepest impression is one that sparks fond memories—and nothing will fit the bill quite like a handmade journal of a family's favorite vacation, or a beloved sibling's best year at school, or a grandmother's long-forgotten wedding. If you have a lot of photographs to choose from, choose selectively and choose the best. Interview family and friends, and record their observations and memories of the occasion you are commemorating. Tell a story with the photos—and if there are several family versions, tell them all. Most photos languish in boxes, improperly preserved and uncataloged. Your journal will revive distant memories, and it will be a gift the recipient will never forget.

Project

PHOTO ALBUM

   a theme
   photo-safe pen
   archival white or off-white acid-free paper, clamshell box,
      or photo album from a photo-supply shop
   archival-quality corners

   Start chronologically and place two or three photos on the right-hand side of each page, allowing enough space for handwritten comments. Try to identify who is in each picture and interview them, or someone who remembers them, about the occasion—quotes are always interesting. You may also want to include other mementos (pressed flowers, invitations, tickets, or programs) in your album.

   If you want to make your own slipcover for the album, follow the directions for "Make a Book Slipcover" on p. 58.

Cut Your Own Christmas Tree

OR MANY PEOPLE the holidays begin the minute they select their tree. This year, rather than purchasing your tree at a store, make an excursion into the countryside to cut your tree at a tree plantation. Take a friend, take your parents, take some children, and arm yourself with warm clothes, a tape measure, and a saw. You might even decide to pack a picnic basket or a thermos steaming with warm soup.

When selecting a tree, look for pliable branches, green needles, and a trunk that is sticky with sap. Once you get your tree home, keep it in a pail of water until you set it up, and then give it up to two quarts of water a day.